MW01273464

Writer: Carola Schmidt
Illustrator: Rafael Antonio
Proofreaders: Christina Ammari and Robert Janelle

All rights reserved. No part of this book may be reproduced, stored in a retrieval system, or transmitted in any form or by any means, electronic, mechanical, photocopying, recording or otherwise without prior written permission from the authors.

 @_CarolaSchmidt

Cancer is...

To hear about miraculous diets...

And be stalked by people with green juices.

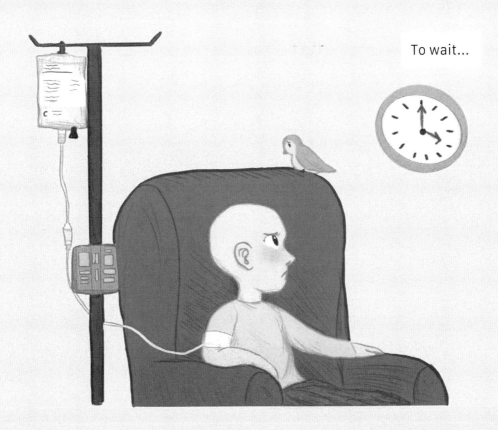

To wait...

Just to wait more.

To secretly fantasize about becoming a superhero during the radiotherapy.

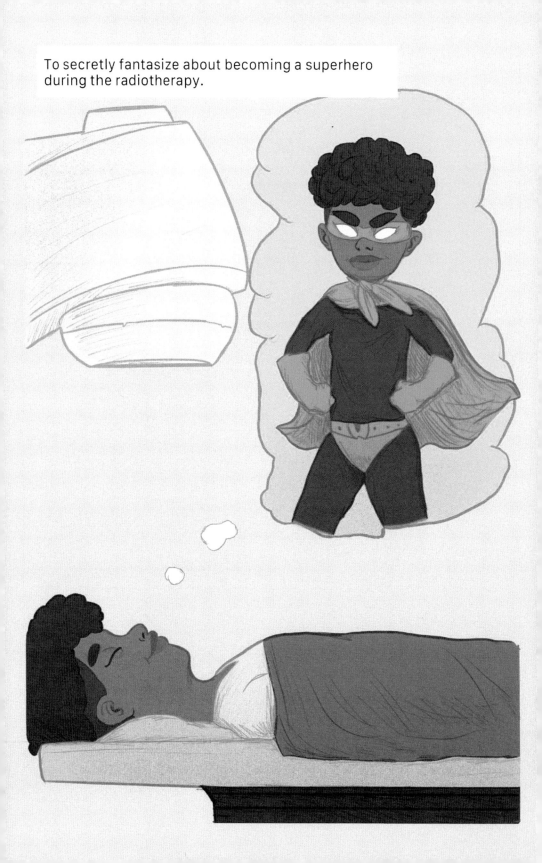

Sometimes, as weird as girls taking a vacation from waxing...

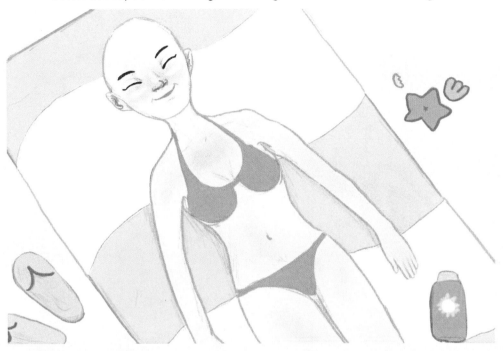

And boys freezing future babies.

To read more about cancer in a day than books in a whole year.

To exchange the ice cream for ginger ice cubes.

To be yourself...

But at the same time, you're someone new.

To be ghosted by some friends...

And meet new ones.

To feel new pains...

But also new joys.

To stop believing in something old...

To believe in something new.

To secretly fantasize about a soundproof mask for a professional who says words you don't like.

To note the nonsense you hear from people with good intentions.

To feel like you don't have to change anything in your habits when a pandemic starts.

To make peace with your hair daily.

To be blamed by toxic people.

To be surprised by sensitive people.

How can I help you today?
Do you need a ride to the chemo?
I can cook for you!

To have a favorite blanket...

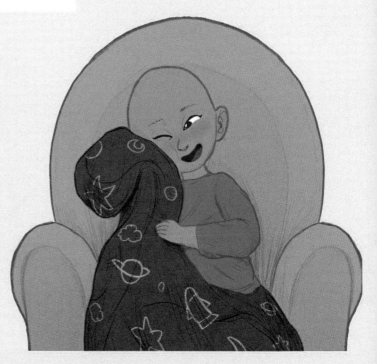

And a favorite hug.

To feel like your pet REALLY understands you.

To burn a best-selling book—about "food to cure cancer!"

Cancer is to realize that sometimes people see you as a brave warrior while others see you as the battlefield.

To feel like only your chemo-friends understand your concern about late effects.

To feel proud of yourself, because YOU SHINE!

Made in the USA
Middletown, DE
06 September 2020

16972638R00018